Worry Reframes
Challenge Your Anxious and
Negative Thoughts!
By Amanda Petrik, LCPC

Dedication
I dedicate this book and owe my
success to my family; Charles and
Helen Petrik (my parents), Jason
Gardner (my husband), Dustin,
Josh, and Ryan Petrik (my three
older brothers) and Molly, Jessica,
and Alyssa Petrik (their amazing
wives). They have provided me
the strength, support, and notion
that I can achieve anything and
help those that need it.

Chapter	Page

Chapter 1
Introduction

Another anxiety self-help book on the market, and you may be wondering, "Why this one and how can it help me?" The evidenced-based treatment for anxiety is called cognitive behavioral therapy (CBT). The idea behind CBT is that our thoughts and feelings are interconnected, meaning your feelings affect your thoughts and your thoughts affect your feelings.

Think about the following scenarios and if you have ever related:

1. It is Sunday evening, and you are already dreading Monday and returning to work. You begin worrying about the amount of work piled up on your desk, the big meeting you have scheduled, whom you will have to interact with, or just the unknown. This list of worries has all of a

sudden ruined your Sunday at home, as you are no longer living in the moment.

2. It is time for your big speech. Despite being well prepared, your mind starts racing with thoughts about forgetting your words, messing up in front of the audience, or wondering if the audience will be bored, laugh, or even make fun of you. Thanks to all of these worries, your heart is now racing and you do not even want to give your speech.

3. Turns out you are human and made a mistake! Maybe it was a mistake on a phone call with a client, a report you wrote, or an email you sent out. Now you are worried how this will impact your job, if others are upset with you, or dwelling on what you should have done instead. These negative thoughts stay with you through the

rest of your workday, impacting not only your productivity but it has also carried on to your home life.

Sound familiar? These are just a few of an unlimited number of examples of how our thoughts can quickly impact our mood. This is where I come in.

A core component of CBT is cognitive restructuring. What is cognitive restructuring and why is it a vital part of treatment? We all have negative thoughts and thought patterns, also known as cognitive distortions. Once we identify these unhelpful thoughts, we can correct or reframe them to improve our mood and anxiety. I am here to help you do this by reframing some of the most common negative thoughts I hear on a daily basis in my work as a therapist.

I am a Licensed Clinical Professional Counselor in the state of Kansas and a Registered Play Therapist-Supervisor, specializing in the treatment of anxiety disorders. I come from a cognitive behavioral theoretical orientation, using cognitive restructuring to assist people just like you and me to challenge our negative thoughts and find a healthier mindset. However, this work is difficult! When our automatic negative thoughts pop into our head, we believe them. We believe they are fact. We believe they are reality. This makes it much more difficult to identify or reframe those thoughts in the moment. I often assist clients in brainstorming more helpful thoughts, but now you have them at the tip of your fingers, whenever needed! This is not a substitute for professional help, if warranted or recommended. This book allows you to perform a necessary step towards a happier, healthier mindset in everyday situations.

Chapter 2
How To Use This Book

I bet you were not expecting to get instructions on how to read a book! I want you to benefit the most from using the information in this book correctly.

The worries and other negative thoughts identified in this book are categorized into separate chapters. These include the general worries that may be seen with Generalized Anxiety, the fear of judgment and scrutiny seen with Social Anxiety, the worries with panic disorder, obsessions found with Obsessive Compulsive Disorder, general negative thoughts found with depression and sadness, and the self-defeating thoughts identified in those with low self-esteem. Feel free to focus on the chapters that relate to your worries or read the entire book from cover to cover to master the technique.

Each thought is presented on one side of the page with the reframes on the other side of the page. This allows you a moment to brainstorm your own reframes before flipping the page. Each thought provides three healthier reframes. Use one, use all three, or come up with one of your own that fits better for you. The goal is to identify a healthier thought that feels comfortable for you, to repeat every time that initial automatic negative thought pops into your head. If you are like most people I have met, you will need to repeat your healthier thought *multiple* times for it to become the new automatic thought.

In addition to repeating the new reframe multiple times, additional tricks I have seen work well for others include:
- Write down your reframe, such as in a journal
- Make it visual, such as on a post-it on your mirror or refrigerator
- Flag the pages in this book with the reframes you need

assistance with most and
re-read them often
- Say them out loud to
yourself and others

Important to note: You will notice that the pronouns, he and she, are used interchangeably throughout the book. Anxiety and negative thoughts impact both genders. Change the pronouns to suit your gender. Also change the thoughts in the book to fit your specific situation. They were written to be as general as possible to apply to everyone and any situation.

Chapter 3
Generalized Anxiety

Generalized Anxiety Disorder (GAD) describes the general worrier whose anxiety and racing thoughts may jump from worry to worry. Today you may worry about your health, tomorrow you worry about your grades or if you will be fired, then your appearance and how you compare to others, then finances, and then your family. These individuals have difficulty controlling the worry, so simply saying "relax" typically does not solve it. Worriers benefit from not only relaxation skills but also learning to manage these anxious thoughts by learning to reframe them in healthier, more helpful ways.

Worry:
What if work is awful tomorrow?

Reframes:
- I am great at my job and prepared for anything that comes at me.
- My day could go like any other day; neither good nor bad.
- I can handle stress if it should come up at work.

Worry:
I fear the unknown.

Reframes:

- The unknown could turn out well. Unknown does not have to be bad.
- Others have this same fear and it would be comforting to talk to them about my feelings.
- I can focus on the present moment, which is actually going quite well.

Worry:
What if she leaves me and I am all
alone?

Reframes:

- She may not even leave me.
- I have others in my life, and I will not be alone.
- I am not reliant on one person. I have many things to be content with in my life including hobbies, work, friends and family.

Worry:
What if there is a
war/tornado/shooting/etc?

Reframes:
- There may not be anything awful that happens.
- Terrible events can happen but I can manage them.
- I can seek support from others if something terrible happens. I will survive.

Worry:
What if I get sick when I go out in
public?

Reframes:

- I may not get sick. I could feel fine.
- I could get sick but no one will notice and I will get through it.
- Maybe others will notice and they will help me or be sympathetic.

Worry:
What if this small pain I am having
is life threatening?

Reframes:

- It is not life threatening and it will go away shortly.
- The pain may need minor attention and treatment, but it is not life threatening.
- It could be an indicator of something more serious, but I am thankful I noticed it so that I can get the proper treatment.

Worry:
What if I never fall asleep tonight?

Reframes:
- I will fall asleep shortly.
- It may take me longer to fall asleep tonight, but I know I eventually will.
- My worry may be causing me to stay up longer, so I will remain hopeful.

Worry:
Am I going to get fired when I go
into work?

Reframes:

- I am not getting fired.
- I will have a good day at work and my boss will be happy with my work.
- I am capable of handling any stress that comes my way at work.

Worry:
Is my friend mad at me? She
hasn't returned my text.

Reframes:
- She has not returned my text because she is busy.
- Her phone could be shut off or the battery has died.
- She may not respond to texts as quickly as I do, but this does not mean she is mad.

Worry:
He's late. Did he get into an
accident?

Reframes:
- He may not have left on time and is running behind.
- He could have run into traffic and that is why he is late.
- He is not as punctual as I am, may have gone to the wrong place, or had to make one more stop before seeing me. There are many possibilities.

Worry:
What if I fail this assignment?

Reframes:

- I will do well on this assignment because I was prepared.
- I may receive an average score, and I will accept that I did my best.
- I may not do as well as I hoped, and I will try again next time.

Worry:
What if I don't make enough
money to survive?

Reframes:

- I may make more money than I need.
- I may make just enough money to get the things in life that I need.
- It may not be as much as I want, but I will work hard, save, and budget in order to live comfortably.

Worry:
What if my first day of
school/work is horrible?

Reframe:

- My first day may go better than I even hoped.
- It could be neutral. My day will be neither good nor bad and I can be okay with that.
- My day may not be as great as I hoped, but I can manage that. Plus, there will be more days to improve from there.

Worry:
What if I am late?

43

Reframes:

- I might be early.
- I could be right on time.
- I may be a little late but people will understand. It happens to everybody.

Chapter 4
Social Anxiety

Social anxiety is a fear of being scrutinized or judged in social situations, fear you will be embarrassed or mess up, or becoming anxious performing in front of others. Those social situations almost always cause anxiety and are often avoided or endured with much displeasure. In children, this anxiety can look like crying, tantrums, clinging, freezing, or not speaking.

Social anxiety is becoming more prevalent in today's world due to advances in technology. Many of our daily activities can be done while avoiding people:

- We can order and deliver our groceries to the door

- Do our shopping online

- Attend meetings via Skype

- Read a book on our phone
  instead of checking it out at
  the library

- Even attend therapy
  sessions online

So when you are required to
interact face-to-face with
another person or perform in front
of a crowd, this can be quite nerve-
wracking. Your thoughts are filled
with worry about what others will
think about you or how you will
perform in front of them.

Worry:
Are they whispering about me?

Reframes:
- They may be discussing something private and sensitive that they do not want anyone to hear about.
- Maybe they did say something about me but it was positive in nature.
- They could be trying to keep their voices down, as not to disturb anyone.

Worry:
Is she looking at me?

Reframes:
- Maybe she is looking at me in a positive manner. For example, she wonders where I got my shirt.
- She may be looking at something next to or behind me but my anxiety assumes it was about me.
- She could be unaware of what she is looking at. She is deep in her own thoughts.

Worry:
Is he judging me?

Reframes:
- He may be thinking positive thoughts about me.
- He may not be thinking about me at all. I'm unable to read minds.
- He may not be fond of me but I do not need to win everyone over. He is allowed to have his thoughts and opinions.

Worry:
Will they laugh at me?

Reframes:
- It will go well and no one will laugh at me.
- People could respond positively, such as with applause or praise.
- It could go even better than planned, and I look forward to doing it again.

Worry:
What if I embarrass myself?

Reframes:
- I will accomplish my task without any shame.
- I could succeed at my task, better than expected, and impress others.
- There is always a chance that something embarrassing in life happens. I will move on from this event.

Worry:
What if I forget what I am going to
say while public speaking?

Reframes:

- I prepared enough and am ready for my speech.
- I might remember the entire speech or can use my notes when needed.
- I can take a few seconds to re-collect myself when needed, and that is okay too.

Worry:
What if I don't know what to say
when talking to someone?

Reframes:
- I will appear confident and carry on an effortless conversation.
- The other person may assist in the conversation, which will help me feel more at ease.
- I will practice some "go to" conversation starters to prepare myself.

Worry:
Will this introduction go badly?

Reframes:
- It could go well and I will meet someone new.
- The person may respond positively, such as with a smile.
- The introduction will be neutral, neither positive nor negative, and that is okay. It is not my job to impress everyone.

Worry:
Will they make fun of me or think I
am "stupid?"

Reframes:

- They may think I am awesome.
- They might be busy with their own thoughts to be worried or judge me.
- They are kind and will not say anything negative to me.

Worry:
What if I get called on in class/the
meeting and I don't know what to
say?

Reframes:

- I might not even get called on.
- I am prepared and ready if I get called on.
- I can take a moment to formulate my response before answering, and that is okay to do.

Worry:
What if I mess up while
performing, such as singing,
playing piano, etc?

Reframes:

- I will do just fine, as I have prepared for this.
- I will do better than expected and will be proud of myself.
- Maybe the audience will respond with applause and be proud of me, no matter how it goes.

Worry:
What if someone else can tell I am
anxious?

Reframes:

- They may not be able to tell, as they cannot read my thoughts.
- They could be anxious too.
- They might be able to tell, but will be supportive and empathetic, which puts me at ease.

Chapter 5
Panic

Panic disorder consists of panic attacks, at times without any predictable trigger beforehand and can occur as often as several times per day or as few as a couple per year. A panic attack lasts approximately 10-15 minutes, is defined as a period of intense fear, and consists of several symptoms such as difficulty breathing, sweating or chills, feeling weak or faint, racing heart, tingling or numbness, chest pains, feelings of choking, nausea, fear of dying, or feeling a loss of control.

The difference between experiencing panic attacks and having a diagnosis of panic disorder is a worry that you will then have additional panic attacks in the future and making changes in your life in fear that you will have another. You may find yourself having such intense anxiety about having a panic attack

that this actually increases the
number of panic attacks you have.

Worry:
What if I have or am having a heart
attack?

Reframes:

- I am just fine. My heart is only racing.
- It feels worse than it is because I am anxious, but my heart rate is actually what it should be.
- A panic attack looks and feels similar to a heart attack, but I can remember that this is my anxiety and it will not hurt me.

Worry:
What if I have another panic
attack?

Reframes:

- I may not have another panic attack.
- I may eventually have another panic attack but I am prepared and can manage it.
- I can utilize healthier, more helpful thoughts, which can actually reduce the number of panic attacks I have.

Worry:
What if I vomit while having a
panic attack?

Reframes:

- I may not vomit. My stomach hurts because I am anxious.
- I will feel better shortly.
- I can use calming techniques to decrease my nausea.

Worry:
What if I faint?

Reframes:

- I can use deep breathing through the panic attack and will not faint.
- I may feel lightheaded but will not faint.
- I will feel better shortly.

Worry:
What if I panic and can't find help?

Reframes:
- I will be able to find help if I need it.
- I will be able to manage my anxious feelings and will not need assistance.
- I may not even panic.

Worry:
What if I die from a panic attack?

Reframes:

- There's a chance I feel sick during my panic attack, but I will not die from it.
- If I feel anxious, I will remember that anxiety does not hurt me.
- My anxiety will decrease shortly, and I will remind myself once again that I can survive these feelings.

Worry:
What if I stop breathing?

Reframes:
- I could have difficulty catching my breath, but I will not stop breathing.
- I may not even have breathing difficulties when I become anxious.
- I can use my diaphragmatic breathing to slow down and regain my breath.

Worry:
What if I panic and can't get out of
here?

Reframes:
- I may not even panic.
- I can manage my panic attack and will not need to escape.
- I may feel anxious and others can assist me if I need help.

Worry:
What if I lose control of myself?

Reframes:
- I will have complete control of myself.
- I could experience slight disassociation (feeling outside of my own body), however I am still in control of my actions.
- I can use calming skills, such as diaphragmatic breathing, to ground myself.

Worry:
What if I never stop shaking?

Reframes:

- I may not even shake this time when anxious.
- Even if I do start shaking, I know it will eventually stop as my body calms down.
- I am able to calm my body even quicker using progressive muscle relaxation techniques.

Chapter 6
Obsessive Compulsive Disorder

Do you ever feel like things "just aren't right" or maybe thoughts get stuck in your head and become distressing? Obsessive Compulsive Disorder (OCD) consists of two parts: Obsessions are the intrusive, persistent and unwanted thoughts or images that get stuck in your head, while the compulsions are the repetitive rituals (or behaviors) you feel you have to complete in order to relieve your anxiety. Some common examples are fear of contamination so you may excessively clean, order and arrange items, check if something has been completed such as if lights are turned off, count items or patterns, or repeat a task multiple times until it is just right or a certain number of times. Some clients report religious obsessions or rituals such as needing to say their prayer a certain number of times or they worry something bad will happen, thoughts of harming someone, disturbing

images of death or grotesque
scenes, or what they feel is
inappropriate sexual thoughts.

Worry:
What if these obsessions never
stop?

Reframes:
- The obsessions may decrease or even stop as I utilize this cognitive restructuring technique.
- I can decide to seek professional treatment if the obsessions do not decrease, and I can get further help there. This includes Exposure & Response Prevention.
- My obsessions may stop or decrease on their own over time.

Worry:
What if my routine does not go as
planned?

Reframes:
- It may not go as planned but I can manage that.
- My routine may go as planned.
- Some parts of my routine may go as planned, but there might be some changes than I can handle.

Worry:
What if something bad happens
because I did not check the locks
once more?

Reframes:
- I will lock the door once and walk away. Most likely nothing bad will happen.
- I can decrease the number of times I check on my locks each day. This will decrease my worry that something bad will happen.
- In the chance something bad does happen, it is not because I did not repeat my compulsion again. Unfortunately bad events can happen to anyone.

Worry:
What if these items are not in
order how I like it?

Reframes:
- I can learn to handle the stress of these items being out of order.
- I can move one thing out of place at a time to slowly manage small changes.
- Many things in my life will not go "how I like it." I can learn how to tolerate these uncomfortable feelings.

Worry:
What if I catch a disease or germs
from touching something dirty?

Reframes:
- I may not catch anything from touching that dirty object.
- There is always a chance I get sick, but excessively washing in fear of contamination is actually worsening my immune system.
- I can find an appropriate balance of when to wash my hands, such as after using the restroom or before dinner, versus when it is not needed.

Worry:
What if something bad happens
because I did not say my prayer
perfectly?

Reframes:

- I can say my prayer imperfectly and see that nothing bad will happen.
- I can continue practicing saying my prayers in different ways to decrease this fear that it has to be perfect.
- There is always a chance that something bad could happen but it is not due to me saying my prayer imperfectly. Unfortunately, bad things can happen to anyone.

Worry:
Did I do a good job?

Reframes:

- I can reassure myself that I did well, and that will mean more than coming from anyone else.
- I did the job to the best of my abilities.
- I can review step-by-step the effort I put into this task and identify one piece I did well at.

Worry:
What if I throw something away
and I need it later?

Reframes:
- I may throw something away and not need it later.
- I can throw it away and be able to replace it later if needed.
- There may be another reason I am holding onto this item, which does not involve the actual physical or monetary value of it. I may be able to resolve what this item is doing for me and be able to let it go.

Worry:
Is this perfectly even or lined up
correctly?

Reframes:
- It may not be perfect but I can manage that anxiety.
- It may not be as I would like but I realize that I can handle that imperfection.
- While this time it might be perfect, I know I cannot always expect it to be.

Worry:
Am I a horrible person for having
bad thoughts about taboo
subjects?

Reframes:
- Everyone has thoughts of a taboo nature from time to time. This does not make me a bad person.
- I can speak to others openly and honestly about my thoughts to receive validation that most people have had these same thoughts at some point.
- My thoughts do not make me a bad person. I do not have control over them. However, I do have control over my actions.

Chapter 7
Depression

Depression is categorized as a mood disorder, causing feelings of sadness, and possible symptoms of hopelessness, worthlessness, changes in appetite, sleep or weight, loss of interest or pleasure in activities, lack of motivation, fatigue, and/or suicidal thoughts. There are many causes or factors, which contribute to depression including genetics, life stressors, medications, and having a condition that often occurs alongside with depression, such as anxiety or substance abuse. Negative thought patterns accompany sadness, such as thoughts of hopelessness, disqualifying the positives, and disappointment when not meeting expectations. Correcting these faulty thought patterns could relieve sadness.

Worry:
I have no motivation to do
anything.

Reframes:
- My motivation may increase after I engage in the task.
- My motivation may come later. It is okay that I lack motivation now and then.
- I can find ways to increase my motivation, such as breaking down a task into smaller steps, asking others to support me, or thinking about the rewards in the end.

Worry:
What if it never gets better?

Reframes:

- I am unable to predict the future. My situation could always improve.
- It will get better but it may take time, effort, and hope.
- Everyone goes through struggles at some point in their life. This may be mine. I will get through it and come out stronger in the end.

Worry:
I have no one.

Reframes:
- I can actually identify many people that care about me.
- I have friends, family, co-workers, and acquaintances that would support me if I called on them.
- There are people I have impacted by my kindness, even if I am not aware of it.

Worry:
I fail at everything.

Reframes:

- I can identify many things I have accomplished, whether at school, work, around the home, in relationships, or with my hobbies.
- I have succeeded at multiple things, though I am currently only seeing the negatives since I am feeling down.
- I do well at some things and don't do well at others. That makes me human.

Worry:
Why did this happen to me?

Reframes:
- Stressful events happen to everyone at some point in their lives. This was not the result of me being a bad person or deserving of something bad.
- What happened was the result of a chain of events. I can look back at the events and see what initiated this to happen.
- Maybe there is no explanation for why this happened but I can focus on how I will manage this or what I learned from it.

Worry:
I should have known better.

Reframes:

- I can learn from my experience.
- I will focus on the present moment and do the best I can from this point on.
- I can give myself compassion and realize that I did the best that I could at the time, with the information I had.

Worry:
What if I never achieve what I
want to achieve?

Reframes:

- I may achieve exactly what I am hoping to achieve.
- My goals may change as I am working towards them, and may achieve something different than originally expected.
- I will try my best towards my goals, and that is all that matters.

Worry:
It was all my fault.

Reframes:

- There may be other factors that were the cause of the issue.
- I can take some responsibility for what happened, but not 100%.
- I can take the majority of the fault and learn from what happened.

Worry:
What if I never meet someone?

Reframes:

- I will meet someone that I spend my life with.
- I can focus my time on other priorities like education or career now, and will meet someone at a later time.
- I may meet someone tomorrow; maybe in a year. Until then I will spend time with family and friends that also love me.

Worry:
I can't do anything right.

Reframes:
- I do many tasks right every day, however my depression is causing me to focus on the things I do not right now.
- While I do make some mistakes, I can learn from them.
- I can identify one thing I have done well right now which will boost my mood.

Chapter 8
Self-Esteem

Self-esteem is the evaluation of our worth and is highly dependent on our positive or negative thoughts about ourselves. How we view ourselves is a combination of our achievements, characteristics we obtain, strengths and talents, or what we can offer to society, impacting if we feel either better or worse about ourselves as a person. Many negative thoughts accompany low self-esteem, such as a skewed view of who cares for us, what we are good at, and disqualifying our strengths. The first step in boosting our self-esteem is improving these positive thoughts about ourselves.

Worry:
I'm not good at anything.

Reframes:

- I can name a couple things I have done well at in my lifetime.
- I'm good at several things even though it may be difficult to see while focusing on the negative.
- I can ask someone I love what I'm good at, to help me through this difficult time.

Worry:
Nobody loves me.

Reframes:
- There are several people that love/care about me; family members, friends, co-workers.
- I can identify at least one person right now that loves me.
- I may need a reminder of everyone that loves me. I can scroll through my photo albums and pictures, phone, social media, address book, etc.

Worry:
I'm always to blame.

Reframes:
- There are other explanations for what happened.
- I may have played a part in what happened in addition to other factors, but I cannot take full responsibility.
- There are times that I make mistakes, but that makes me a human. I will learn from that.

Worry:
I should have done better,
performed better, or known better.

Reframes:
- I did what I thought was right.
- I performed my best.
- I can learn from what happened.

Worry:
What if he does not like me?

Reframes:
- He may like me. I cannot read his mind.
- I will not be able to tell if he likes me until he says so or I ask. I cannot make assumptions.
- Even if he does not like me, I can handle that. It is not my job to make everyone like me in life.

Worry:
I don't deserve good things in life.

Reframes:

- I do deserve good things, as everyone does.
- I am feeling unworthy of good things because I feel down, but this does not mean I am not deserving.
- I am not seeing all of the good things that have already happened in my life.

Worry:
She is much prettier than I am.

Reframes:
- We both have strengths in our physical appearance.
- We have strengths in different areas and we cannot compare ourselves to each other.
- People have different ideas of what "pretty" is. There is no way to compare.

Worry:
I will never be as good as she.

Reframes:
- There are many things that I do well. There are many things that she does well. We cannot compare the two of us.
- I am having trouble remembering the many good things I have done because I am feeling down. That does not mean they are not there.
- I can identify right now all the things I have done right today.

Worry:
He only complimented me because
he was being nice.

Reframes:

- He complimented me because he meant it.
- He may have complimented me because he is nice, but that does not mean he did not mean it as well.
- A compliment is positive and does great things for my mood either way.

Worry:
I am stupid/a
disappointment/worthless.

Reframes:
- I am a good person with good qualities.
- I can identify more positive labels about myself, as these will produce more positive feelings about myself.
- I can describe the situation that led to these labels, as we are all human, with mistakes, flaws, and stories to tell. That does not mean we do not have a good qualities as well.

Chapter 9
What's Next?

One of my complaints both as a therapist and as an individual with negative thoughts just like you is hearing "be positive" or "think happy thoughts." While this is the right concept, I wish it were that easy. However you have now taken the appropriate steps with this book to get there. Whether you identify with the thoughts listed in this book or identified new ones, the first step is to be aware of what is causing that negative feeling in your head and body. Now you are on your way to brainstorming healthier reframes. Find the reframe (or pick multiple ones) that feels the most natural and believable for you, and begin repeating…and repeating…and repeating. Replace your old thought with your new reframe each and every time it pops up. Soon, you will "be positive" and "think happy thoughts," thanks to the effort and time you put into your mental health.